Mountain Spirits Speak

A Spiritual Encounter

by J. L. Baumann

Ex Libris

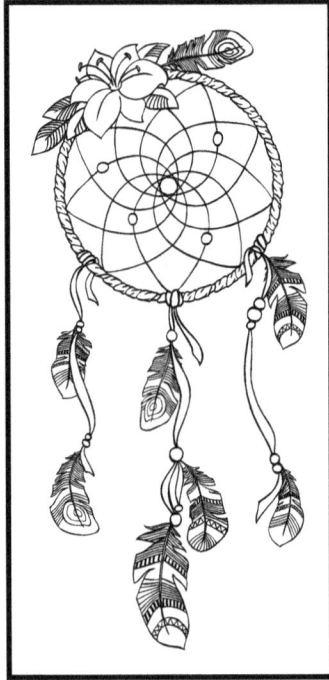

Name_____

Date_____

Printed in The United States of America
Link Printing, Groveland, Florida 34736

~ *For* ~
Robin Varner

ISBN 978-1-941880-20-3

~ First Edition ~

Table of Contents

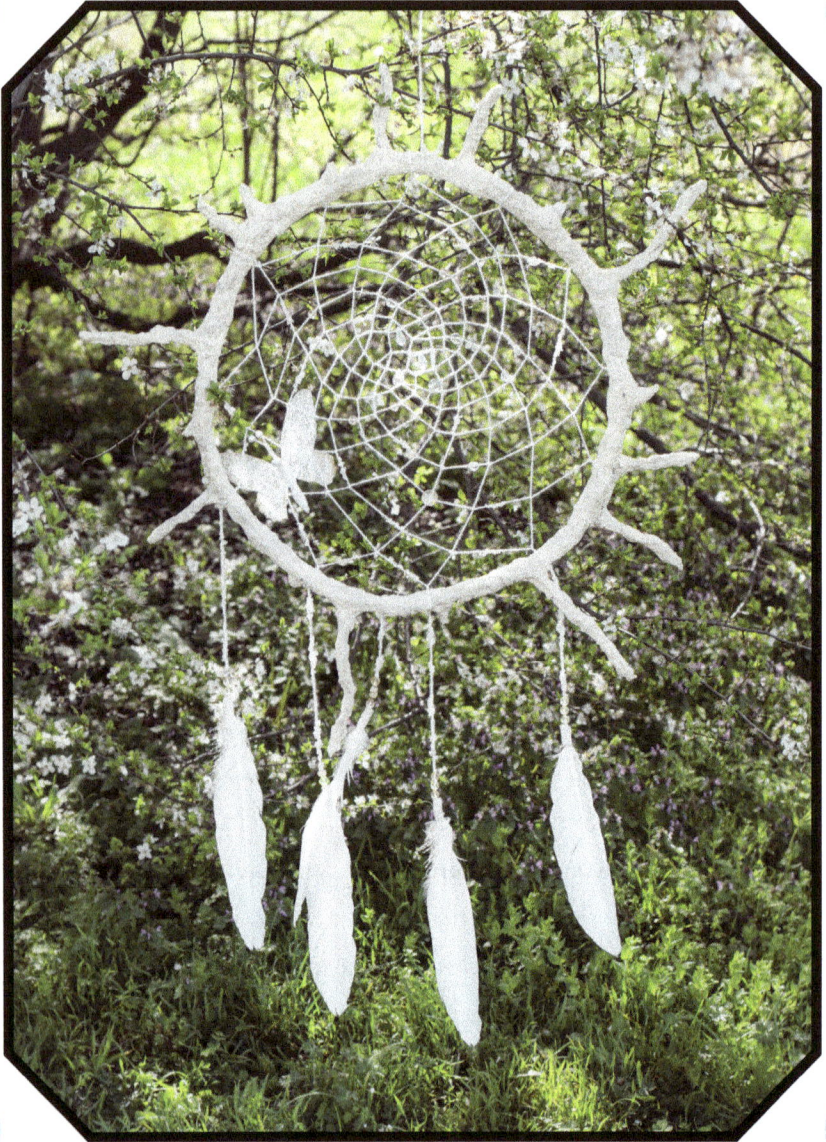

The Fortunes of Faith

You can't hide from me, the wise old shaman said
For J am your reality when J'm inside your head
You think you're all alone, when no one is around
But surely it is known, J can move without a sound

Sometimes J am a twitch, that cannot be explained
Sometimes J am that itch, that drives us all insane
Perchance J am the spirit, that treats you in despair
Perhaps you cannot hear it, but feel that J am there

J'm also there in happiness, escorting your elation
Abating all your sadness, by instilling inspiration
To see beyond the trivial, to all that is worthwhile
And be beyond the physical, the essence of a smile

So dream a dream worth catchin, in quiet solitude
And J'll reward your passion, at our next interlude

The Rewards of Love

It's nice to be in love with spring
To find the love in everything
Like feelings never felt before
The joy of youth upon your door

The summer sun bakes in the truth
That love goes on and passes youth
You know that love's the reason why
And pray that it will never die

Fall comes along with certitude
And love's true colors we conclude
Gives brilliance to our lives
And humbly hope as time goes by

When winter comes with its repose
A song of love will be composed

The Elf and the Robin

The elf and the robin made a pact
Beneath the blooming dogwood tree
Beneath its all white canopy
They sealed it with a kiss

Now the petals of white,
In the bright sunlight
Had all called out in sheer delight
Seal it with a kiss

As the flowers fluttered in the gentle breeze
And the meadow buzzed with bumblebees
Another kiss is what you need
And they all agreed, it had to be

So from one to another, they kissed again
To forever together belong

For she had the magic of life in her
And he had the magic of song

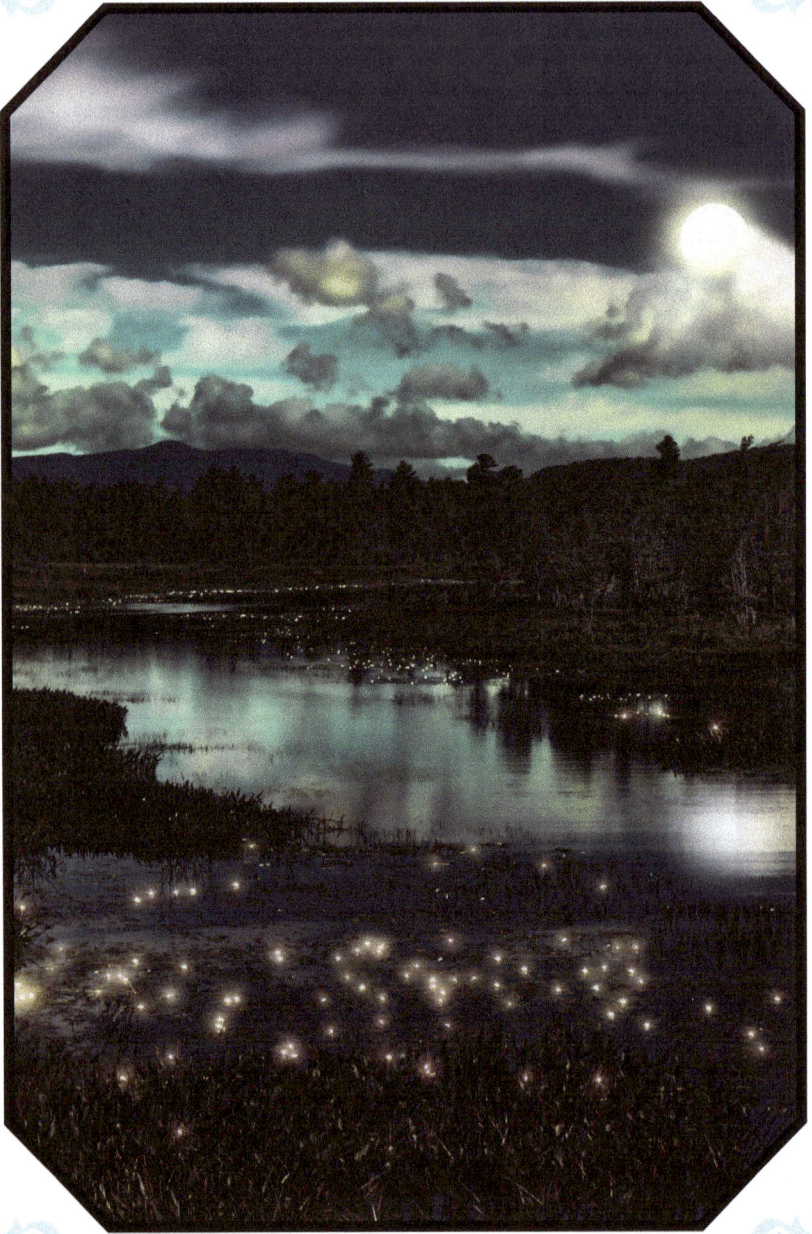

Natural Predators

I'm just a little firefly that's trying to stay alive
It isn't hard to understand
Just why I fly at night

When all the birdies of the day are finally asleep
I take my lantern out to play
Lighting up the street

So happily I fly along to brighten up the night
Not fearing to be eaten now
While I am in mid flight

But my light is not forever, as is the moon and stars
Knowing I might be entrapped
By little kids with jars

Guests

As Jack Frost skates on rural lanes
And Frosty rules the snow's domain
While Old Man Winter freezes rain
You think of springtime once again

When little fairies flit and fly
As farmers sow their corn and rye
The dormant spirits come alive
To play in rushing brooks nearby

As summer trees shade Elvin Kings
An errant Bard gives song to things
That o'er the farm and fields do sing
Of all the cheer their harvest brings

When orange leaves begin to fall
Forget us not, the fairies call
Our spirits big, tho we be small
And we'll return to dust you all

So don't be sad, it's not the end
For soon you will see Jack again

Tempus Fugit

As beauty is love for all to have and hold
A single thought, unique to one's own soul
It takes away a young man's breath to see
A summer cotton dress that flutters aimlessly

Oh Wind, you know exactly what you do
To give a man such passion he'll pursue
The sound of laughter and a sunny smile
To chase a dream, his very will beguiled

With hopes of being caught she flits along
With flowers in her hair she sings her song
To consummate her purpose is her goal
With love and tenderness to make her whole

Look now! A sprite has beckoned unto me
Before she fades away this day for all eternity

Snowflakes in the Air

I love the snow, it's made of tiny souls
Crystalized in flakes from angel tears
They're young and old and do behold
The thoughts of everyone in silence
As quietly they float about in time
Sublime in purity, immune to woe

Falsely, they're not driven by the wind
As if the wind controls their destiny
For souls exist wherever souls exist
Their presence be not tangible to see
They are the essence of a snowflake
A commodity worth nothing in the air
Except for children's noses to discover
And memories of other cherished times
These nano souls appear and reappear
And year to year they seem to reaffirm
They just become a part of us as such

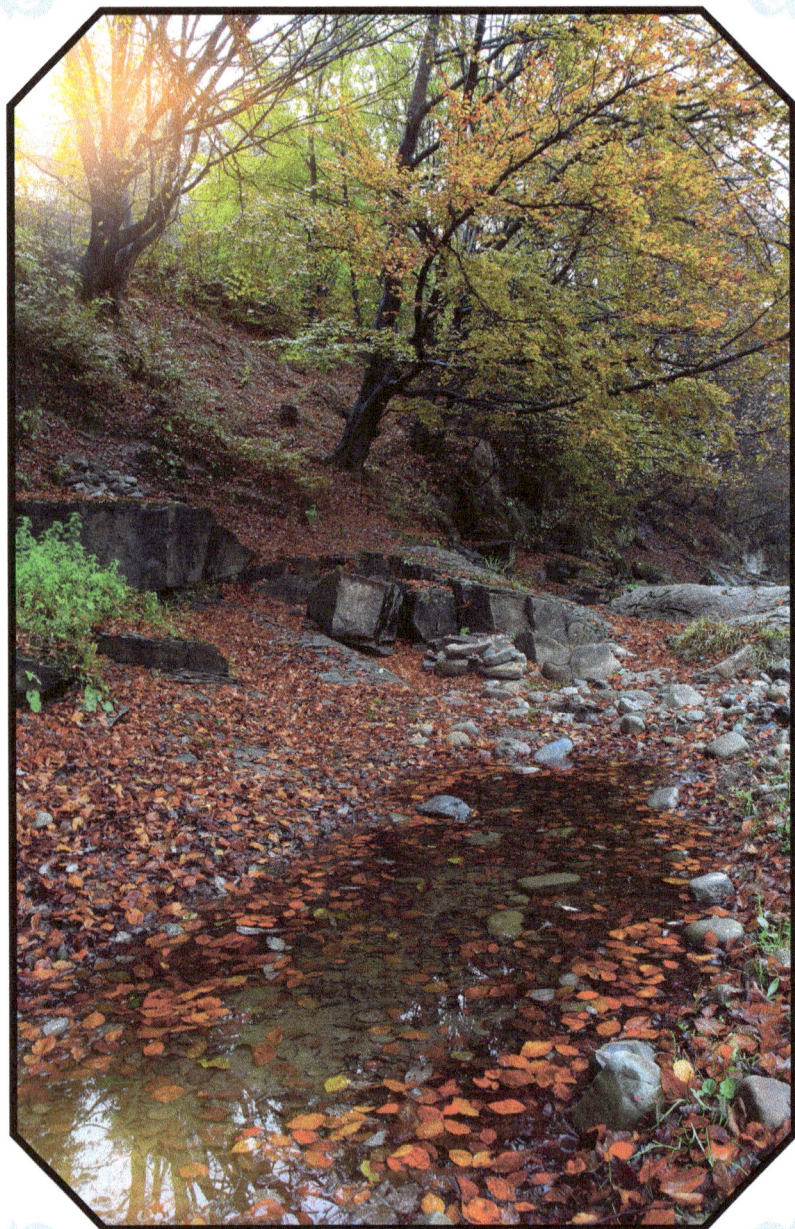

Indian Summer

She is the unexpected rustle in the leaves
She is the witness to the hardwood trees
She is the shadow cast by fleeting birds
She is the calling, speaking not in words

She is the sunshine, bearing love itself
She is the scent that flowers by herself
She is the trickle underneath the brook
She is the necessary time it took to look

She is the earth, the very earth you plow
She is the sky behind the summer cloud
She is the faith that fosters all serenity
She is the grace of mountains' majesty

She is the robin that appears in spring
She is the reason that we do our thing

Homeward Bound

Into the crowded city I went, to find myself alone
Adventure was my sole intent, a taste of the unknown
I left the mountain's sanctity, born within my soul
To seek out God's humanity, his multitudes extolled

Finally, I had arrived, where nary a tree did stand
For not a single one survived, the city's callous plan
The folks went on efficiently, seeking only pleasure
Praying most deficiently, to gold and silver treasure

The valley's crystal brooks were turned into a sewer
And without their natural babble, gone was the allure
Vapid was the slightest breeze, of jasmine scented air
As animals are tagged and leashed, in city doctrinaire

For adventures are a curious thing, a mountain of a task
Returning home you realize, you can't escape your past

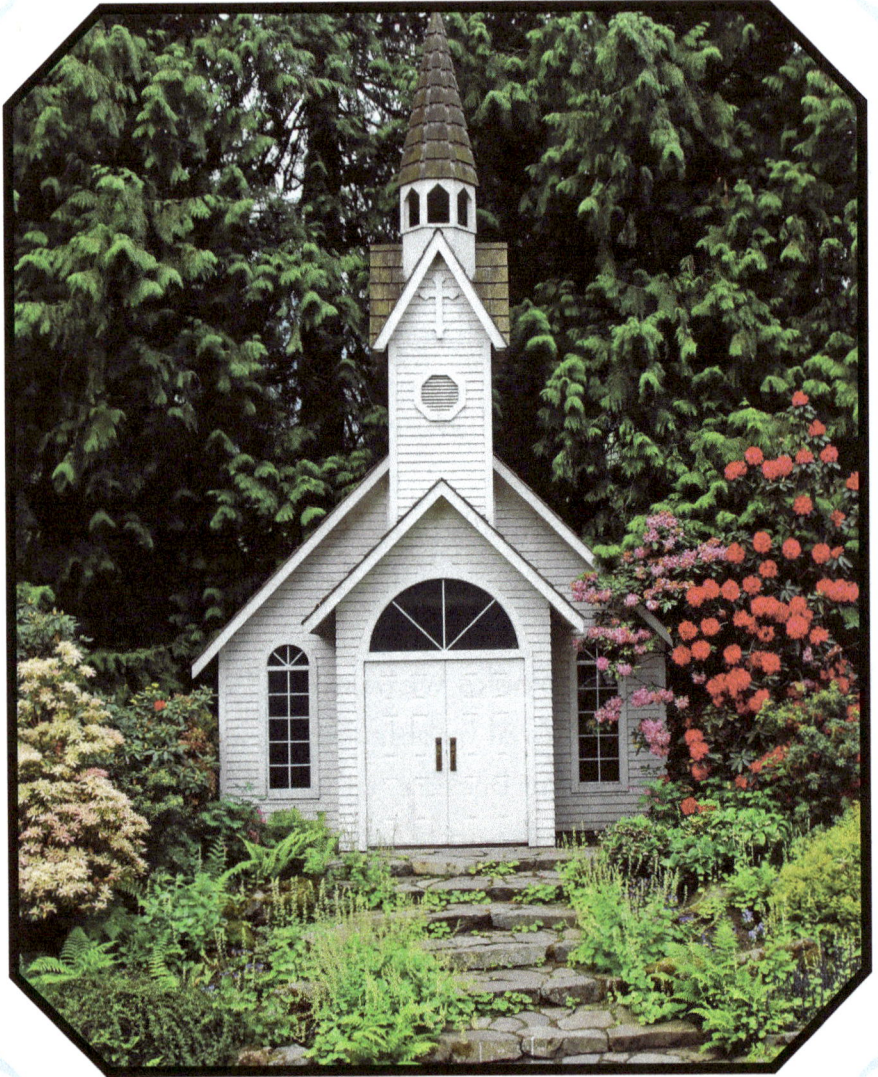

Complete Surrender

It is your love that makes me feel alive
Your tender kisses weaken me inside
As I surrender to your soft caress
My heart's forever yours I must confess

You took me by surprise as I gave in
To wanton feelings I had hid within
So now I'm paralyzed and naked too
And all because I fell in love with you

My passion has consumed my very soul
To once again love you, my only goal
Take me now, don't leave me in this way
To not receive the rapture of the day

Your love's a pleasure I can't live without
You are my love and all that I'm about

A Cherokee Valentine

Sometimes I wonder whether,
    if I only had one feather, could I fly?
If I waved it all around,
    will I get up off the ground, and should I try?
Do I spin it round and round,
    and as I flap it up and down, do I pray?
And so I wonder altogether,
    am I really all that cleaver, here today?

    I think I need a second feather!

A Summer's Eve

As one surveys the sunset's creamy crimson skies
That had caught the night before it closed eyes
And just when its eastern half
Had turned the swirling clouds at last
Into a faded hue of royal blue
It left then there to dissipate and die
And in life's vanity you wonder why

A Full Palette

Life explodes in a blinding white
From the colorless void we come
Conceived beyond our very sight
The void's remanded to succumb

Then yellow bursts upon the scene
With vibrant beams of golden light
The breath of life inside does seem
To warm us with a God's delight

Midst orange flairs and scarlet red
We touch the heaven's surly might
With caution gone we surely tread
Convinced we truly have the right

When green's sereneness filters in
No longer are you bound so tight
You now express the soul within
And redefine your natural plight

Enjoy the blues with all their hues
They're comforting but not as bright
Revere the past and sit and muse
For nature's peace you now invite

As royal shades of purple fade
And candles flicker in the night
My colored life I'd never change
For me it's been a true delight

Tanasqui

You feel the blues of a misty mountain's high
See a heaven's rainbow consecrate your eyes
Touch the natural independence of your soul
Absorb a crystal droplet as it waterfalls below

Cry not for Choctaw, Chickasaw or Cherokee
Their spirits dwell as fireflies for all eternity
Directing streams and rivulets to all converge
In irised valleys supervised by mockingbirds

Rivers roar relentlessly, defining immortality
Pled in terms which only recognize humility
You listen quietly to know why you are here
And discover your self-dignity and volunteer

In a state of grace, bestowed most naturally
You embrace the spirit that is Tennessee

Nighty Night

First it comes as a whisper, carried by the winds of time
Enticingly the great elixir, calls unto thee to be entwined
In cosmic skies enshrined, in heaven's will to be nobility
In all things past or yet to be, embracing infinite capacity

As twilight time evokes an apprehensive contemplation
Vesperically you wonder, beseeching mortal vindication
In the dissipation of the day, surrendering its dominance
In natural gracious dignity, yielding all preponderance

Patiently you dwell amidst the ambiance of dusky lights
And contemplate the vagueness of your nugatory plight
You welcome time to whisk away the clutter all around
To take advantage of the night, to gain insight profound

Then clarity in flecks appear against the pitch black sky
You surrender unto Morpheus in hope you'll be revived

Wholly in Love

For I had been empty
I could no longer pretend
For I did not understand
And could not comprehend
The instant you took me
There was nothing inside
But you gave me a passion
I could no longer hide

For only to love you, is all that I feel
For I love you completely and surrender my soul
The moment I saw you I knew it was real
That we would be lovers, that we would be whole

I feel you inside me
You will never be gone
For lying beside me
Is a beautiful song
To have and to hold
Is my only desire
For your love I behold
Is what gives me my fire

For only to love you, is all that I feel
For I love you completely and surrender my soul
The moment I saw you I knew it was real
That we would be lovers, that we would be whole

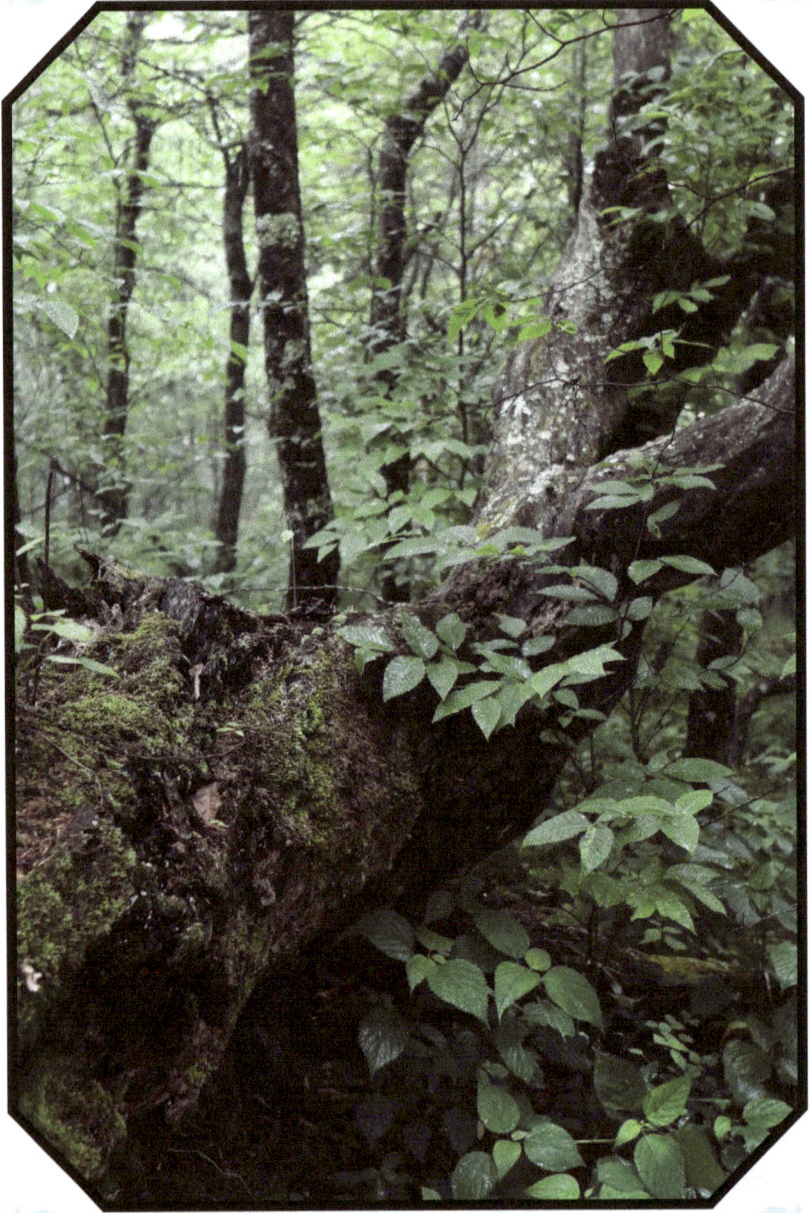

Grave Considerations

I sat alone on a fallen tree that lay beside the trail
Do you mind me resting here? I asked to no avail
You surely were a mighty one, I complimented so
But still it did not answer, so I politely did not go

This summer seems a hot one, I testified out loud
When all I heard was solitude, whispering around
I decided it was comfortable, a sitting on that tree
But still this fallen tree, would yet not answer me

Do many come to sit here? I asked that sunny day
To ponder reverently, how it came to be this way
That I should rest upon you, lying on this ground
Accommodating graciously, not uttering a sound

I feel you still can hear me, for spirits do not pass
So when the acorn hit me, you spoke to me at last

The Snowman Cometh

The sky is lit in twinkling lights of fragile thoughts of hope
Glistening o'er a snow so bright, as snowflakes verily elope
With childhood dreams that reappear, joyously in splendor
Awakening those days of old, all but forgotten in surrender

Innocence is never lost, becoming dormant in compliance
Initially a thaw is felt, confronting now your own defiance
Embrace the snowy angels, resurrect your childhood past
Reject that merry old snowmen are never expected to last

Christmas carols call to thee, to now surrender reverently
Renounce the chaos that you see, seek virtue in simplicity
Rejoice the vestal nature of a child, God's gift you can revive
And certify to all who'll listen, that snowmen are indeed alive

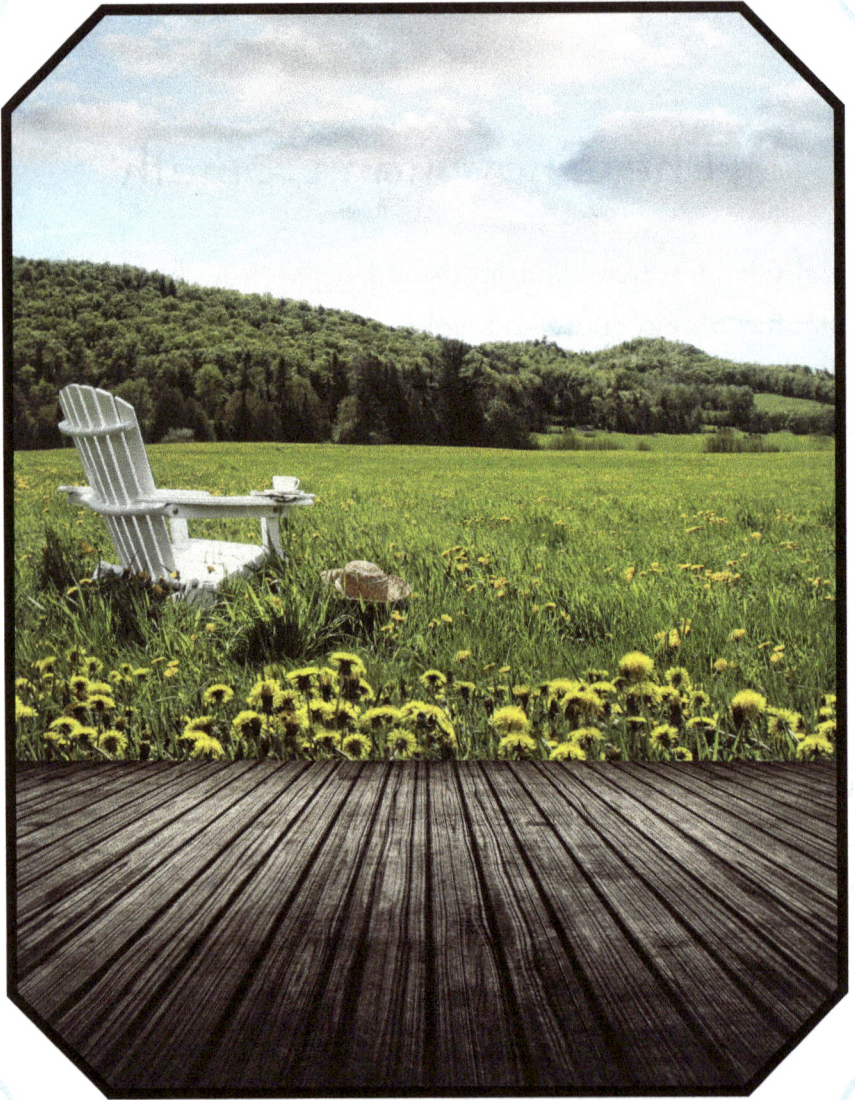

A Warm Proposition

Speak not of pleasures past as only memories
They rule the reason why you must proceed
Provoking you to love the smallest of all things
Like sunshine on your face that comes in spring

Appreciate the reason why you age like wine
So drink again and drink again, until your time
Familiar in the fact, you know the reason why
Your memories give you a reason to survive

Forget me not, forget me not, they all but cry
When a mother begs another child come alive
Knowing she won't smother other memories
For new ones only help the old ones breathe

So come with me where memories are made
And the sunshine on your face will never fade

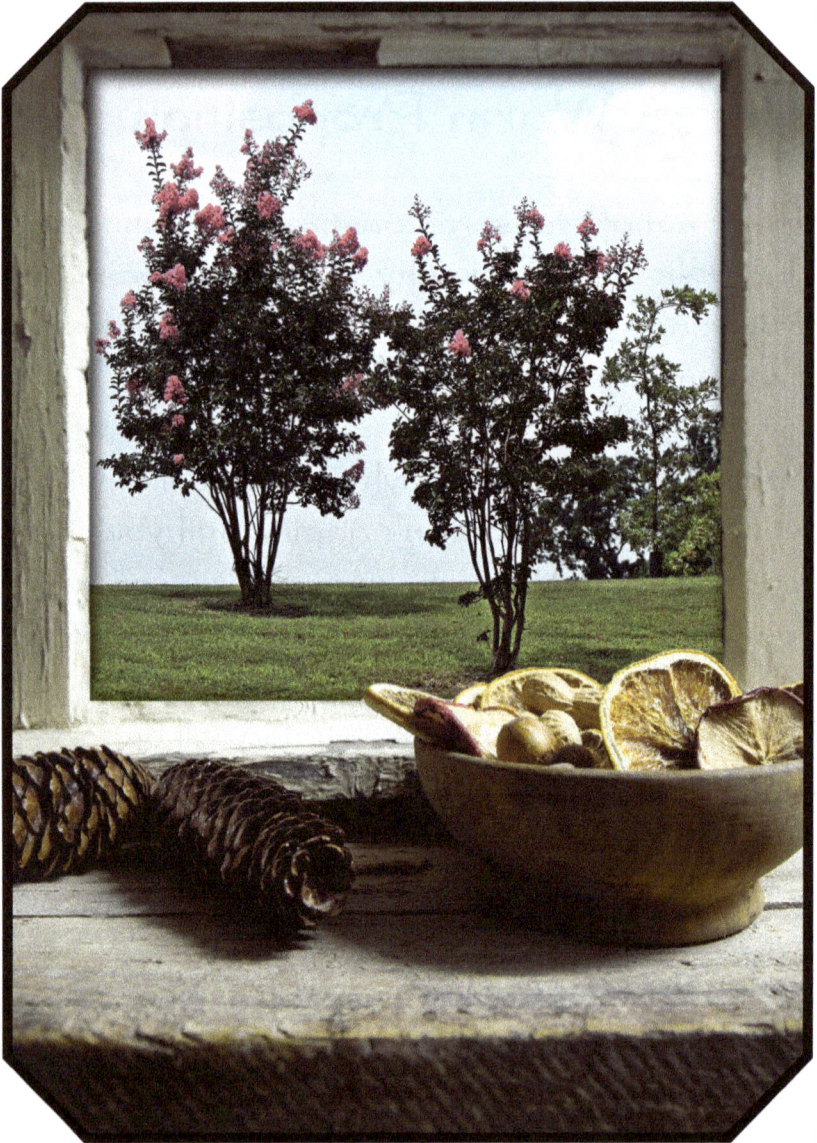

Outside My Window Frame

Myrtle, why do you flower before me, outside my window frame
In pink and white and red, for me to see your love so unashamed
The more you're pruned, the more you seem to bloom with pride
As if you have assumed the right, to now demand I come outside
Perhaps you had no choice, to feel you were compelled to bloom
To signify propitiously that summer justifies the adolescent June
Stark and bright you challenge me to keep the promises of spring
That in the garden of our youth we had acknowledged everything

In fullest bloom and variegated colors the summer heat called out
Experience her splendor, and you will find out what it's all about
Abandoning my window, I couldn't sit and watch her silent tease
I had to brave the heat and view her clearly bending in the breeze
And so alas, when her summer's past, I now declare and validate
That when her flowers go to fall, I won't forget my summer date

My Natural Wood Burning Fire

I wasn't cold, but still I built a fire, an awesome all-consuming fire
That beckoned me to sit a while and keep it company

It took some time to talk to me, and felt it tried to comfort me
And make me smile inwardly, as patiently I waited

And so it was, just me and the fire, and the fire's desire
To keep my thoughts from wandering away

As it bade me not to stray, now calling out in a bold display
With a flurry of sparks in disarray, I felt it say, tranquility

So I leaned on back, to watch a while, and ponder its advice
And watched it settle down, to now ponder its demise

As one by one, the logs retired, creating its own funeral pyre
Its embers declared to me from the fire, I am tranquility

A Winter's Kiss

When the flurries of the first fallen snow begin to appear
It begins and marks the start of all that will be inevitable
Provoking comfort in the familiar sense of things sublime
That wisp and whirl about unto the panorama of your eyes
As a barrage of tiny snowflakes dance wildly in the wind
Crisp and clean, you breathe it in, the essence of existence
Intermittently they land upon your face like tiny seraphim
Who kiss your cheeks to test the very warmth within you
Awakening the thought of all the other kisses felt before
While soliciting your treasured memories to beg for more
You stand alone in frozen time against the pitch black sky
For the twinkling stars above have kept you mesmerized
To briefly make you stop and realize the snowflake's fate
Especially all the teeny ones, who wept upon your face
In the completion of their destiny, as it was meant to be
Introspectively, you try to contemplate the inconceivable
And only find the answer lies beyond your mortal acuity
To fathom that defined expectancies are only fantasies
Of which only exist in the fleeting moments of your mind
Attesting to your infinite obscurity, against which you rail
So hail, and hail again, the fragile and tenacious snowflake
That whirls and twirls about in effervescent spontaneity
Provoking all your senses to find a comfort in their quest
To once again present you with that random kiss of joy
As down your cheeks they melt, for you, and you alone

Passion

To feel passion is to taste of the fruits of love
Abandon ye all reason, to fly on winged doves
Taste the essence of ambrosia, sense the dare
You can smell the breath of sunshine in the air
It forces out the loathsome presence of despair

You can see beyond your selfish preservation
Acquire thoughts of ecstasy, be determination
Experience an energy you never knew before
Commit precociously an act you can't afford
Dare to balance trust, submit before the Lord

Understand the gravity that spirits truly fly
Embrace it candidly, your spirit's not inside
It's somewhere out there prodding you to be
An unrestricted spirit, free from all mortality
Denying rules created by mortals of insanity
It calls you now to fly, with sheer impunity

What do they know of passion, all who die?
To only once have had it, is the reason why

Love's Demands

Love is many things, but it is not reality, it is a state of mind
That drives the machinery, the mechanics of dreams, forward
Both a curse and a blessing, love wields its awesome power
Equally transcending all time in a vengeance, second to none
It is the greatest fear in the cosmos, for it cannot be controlled
So insidious, its nature can and has subdued the mightiest of all
Innately born, it can't be barred by knowledge or in ignorance
Even hate can be subdued by love, as fleeting as it seems to be
It appears with no apparent cause, to conquer unequivocally
It can't be taught like hate, to lie and hide in terms of fate
In all its forms it has no shape and no dimension of existence
To make its presence known, evoking passion with impunity
Consequences be damned, as ecstasy is crowned omnipotent
Existentially existing betwixt desire and intellect it osculates
Our senses to spawn compelling action from our dormancy
Giving rise to thoughts of consternation, seeking now to ratify
Your past belief that your nature was content to be in peace
As the exhilaration of its power compromises your integrity
Adrenalized, your mortal being casts off its shackles joyously
From being trapped within its own mortality to rise above itself
And claim the prize of satisfaction to only linger momentarily
Basking in the deceitful afterglow that you have prevailed
In boasting to yourself to have entrapped the elusive love alive
As the folly of your existence makes you shudder deep inside
For kindness is not a quality of love, and neither is endurance
Evading definition while hope, the scourge of man, prods on
The duplicity of which inevitably reveals its merciless ways
Denying everlasting rapture in cloaked amaranthine deception
Duplicity, thy name is mine, love contumaciously propounds
To all who seek a taste come by, to may or not, be recognized
To risk your sacred soul, surrendering your cognitive control
Unto the soul of all who came before and who'll be there after
As I, the love of God, the greatest gift to man, command you
Give unto me assistance, for I alone cannot conceive mortality

Malaise

Pushing up daisies, one by one
Just doesn't seem to be much fun
I want to be on top again
Unfettered, to be naturally free
To cultivate a flowered destiny
To spindle and to bend
In wind and rain and sunny days
To bloom again and be amazed
And now I must contend again
Pushing up daisies one by one
Just doesn't seem to be much fun

www.ingramcontent.com/pod-product-compliance
Lightning Source LLC
Chambersburg PA
CBHW060557100426

42742CB00013B/2601